D1606416

Prairie Schooner Book Prize in Poetry EDITOR HILDA RAZ

Adonis Garage

Rynn Williams

University of Nebraska Press, Lincoln and London

Manufactured in the United States of America ♾
Designed and typeset in Charlotte by Dika Eckersley.
Printed by Edwards Brothers, Inc.
Library of Congress Cataloging-in-Publication Data
Williams, Rynn. Adonis Garage / Rynn Williams
p. cm. "Prairie Schooner Book Prize in Poetry."
ISBN-13: 978-0-8032-9857-6 (pbk.: alk. paper)
ISBN-10: 0-8032-9857-9 (pbk.: alk. paper)
1. Times Square (New York, N.Y.) – Poetry.
I. Title.
PS3623.I5628A66 2005
811'.6 – dc22
2005000675

For Bolivia, Violet, and Beckett

Contents

3

Acknowledgments

I am grateful to the editors of the following journals for publishing these poems:
Field: Contemporary Poetry and Poetics: "Big Yard," "Islands"
The Greensboro Review: "In the Course of Unwinding"
Gulf Stream Magazine: "The Amusement Park"
The Massachusetts Review: "The Patriarch"
National Forum: The Phi Kappa Phi Journal: "Blue Angel" (formerly "The Facelift")
Ninth Letter: "Anniversary"
Pacific Review: "Fierce-Throated Beauty"
Poet Lore: "The Spool"
Prairie Schooner: "Adonis Garage (1978)," "A Door Opens," "Arc of Desire," "Chicken," "Hep C," "2D12365690"
Primavera: "Surrender"
The Seattle Review: "The Sample Makers"
Southern Humanities Review: "Topography"
Swink: "The Forest at the Edge of the World"

Deepest thanks to all the teachers, friends, and family who have supported me as a writer. In particular: Ellen Voigt, Heather McHugh, Brooks Haxton, Amy McNamara, Catherine Barnett, Abby Wender, Susan Bruce, Christina Davis, Miranda Field, and Barbara O'Dair. Much gratitude to Stephen Williams. Thanks to the New York State Foundation for the Arts for financial assistance, and to my mother, Jeannene, for support of all kinds. And because it can never be said enough, thanks to Ellen, again.

Acknowledgments

The Sample Makers

How did they come to the same place, the same skill—
from Italy, from Israel, China and Chile?

The women who worked in the back behind the showroom,
in the overwarm, dustball rooms lit by industrial light,

away from the glamour, back where the gush of steam irons
kept a thin gloss of sweat on neck and brows—

hooks and eyes, mousetraps and the tea water boiling,
women who marked their sewing machines

with statuettes and rosaries, Buddhas and baby pictures,
postcards of mountains and small seaside towns?

Barely understanding each other, but understanding
basting, bobbins and straight pins,

the facing and the grosgrain and the seam allowances.
I worked there, too, every day after school,

taking the same greasy manual elevator, using the same
ribboned ladies room key. They would bring a muslin,

half a dress maybe, and place it, delicately, over my arm.
Someone would fit the bodice around my waist,

mark a new neckline, adjust a sleeve, pin the silk
so that it fit my body—me, the living mannequin

who teetered around them in high heels and panties.
And unlike the other women in my life,

they took my chin in their hands, fed me flan
and cannolis, they beamed and they winked and they wept.

What became of them? What of Marie with her cancerous breast,
stitching her daughter's wedding gown on her lunch hour,

and Lily, the saucy bottle-blond, who nipped at schnapps?
What became of the tiny rose, Lia from Ghana?

I remember their hands: thick molded knuckles,
elegant wrists, short, ridged fingernails.

I thought of them today, in Spring Joy restaurant—
beside a little shrine and an industrial refrigerator,

the flat golden bowl of oil, the floating flower petals
and beatific Buddha—when the clerk gave me my purchase.

She was quiet, you could tell, studious in her own way,
still girlish, as if waiting for someone,

wisps of hair falling into her face—
How do they survive here,
these women with soft, steady bodies and careful hairnets?

Oh little hive in the heat and the dust—
have you kept up the prayers, the garlands of herbs?

Topography

Even my bathroom is papered in maps.
Medieval Paris along the far wall,
the Lone Star State curling, yellowed
from the ceiling, Steinberg's Manhattan
behind the door. You can stand in the shower
with the weight of your life, and travel
the northward surge of the Nile
as it moves toward Khartoum, Luxor, Cairo.

In my hallway: nineteenth-century Amsterdam,
the tiny trees, every branch distinct,
grain of the wood visible, and the paths
among them, stately, converging corridors,
all drawn with the careful precision of an architect,
like my father with his mechanical pencils,
gray gum eraser, protractor, bifocals,
head bent down close to the board.

This map gives my hallway certitude—
mathematical, no room for dispute,
the path of the parson to his parish,
the daily route of merchants, the school children
turning the corner into Noordermarkt
where gabled houses faced the canals
and the draft horses lumbered
up Westerstraat on their way to the ports.

I go there and I trace the trajectories,
the small yellow side streets, safe and ancient,
I follow a path to its clear-cut conclusion,
the perfect circle of the cul-de-sac,
the pristine angles, the arc of the bridge.
I don't know if my father was ever in Amsterdam.
But I think of him, how quietly he walked away from us:
his gabardine trench coat, collar turned up.

The Patriarch

Of course we knew the "incidents," the aura
of Divinity, duck-and-cover in the parking garage,
Gloria Swanson chinchilla redux, yes,
he'd been a bombshell—the eyes still sang
with the merriment of a punchbowl, fine wrists,
that dahlia neck, skin bleached with peroxide,
of course he swam in the nude, stashed gin
in the toilet tank, stored stockings in the freezer
so they wouldn't run, had a thing for Adenauer,
played roulette with the .45 won in a Cuban dancehall,
raging along hallways, fathering four children,
feeling the eyes of the back stairs, beck of the undercurrent,
his own hand in his lap like an orphan,
of course he gardened in Dior, of course he was flagrant,

but what escaped us was the way he peeked
into the neighbor's kitchen drawers for something
he swore they'd stolen, beyond the foreground obligation,
aspiration insistent as a stuck car horn in the slow
blue hours of morning, discarded affection,
what escaped us was the dampness at the collarbone,
the delicacy of the pose (cigarette and upturned cheek),
the lingering by the kitchen knives, the bias cut
of the dressing gown, break and fall, tumbrel of illusion—

and what we wanted to escape: that he was ruthless, beyond hope.

Blue Angel

When I open the door to his apartment, my father
does not turn his head, his neck muffled

in a bright Hermès scarf.
It is winter, heat bangs the pipes—

a whistling hiss from the radiator near the window—
and he is seated on the chaise lounge. In the tiny kitchen,

after I fill his favorite highball glass with ice,
I crack the cap on the Diet Pepsi, which startles him,

he calls out and I answer, coming with a tray.
Next to him on the low table there's a vase

of pastel peonies so full and heady, they're nearly obscene.
I want to move them to the windowsill, but no,

he says they'll wilt in the heat. He says,
I was awake for the whole thing—

and I too hear the snips, the chunk of the staple gun.
His taut cheeks look like the skin on a roast bird,

with livid seams from temple to earlobe,
blood and black thread behind the ears.

So how do I look, he says, with a hand at his hairline.
Like Dietrich in *Blue Angel*, I say, looking down. He laughs,

and winces, reaching into the small pile of Valiums on the tray,
the blue ones, the strong ones, and I see his reflection

in the dark of the window glass, he's watching it,
and watching the lights along the skyline, his eyes

bright as a child's. There's Rocky Road in the freezer,
I tell him, picking one withered petal from its stem.

Beneath the tight head his body seems smaller.
You're a doll, he says, but cannot turn his head

when I lean to kiss him goodbye.

Arc of Desire

It was a kid in the Bronx, barely a teenager,
up around Grand Concourse near Yankee Stadium.
His friends said he was stoned, they all were up there

on the roof, really fucked up, crouched
in a corner out of the wind. It was early spring.
Maybe he started it all on a dare, maybe he stood up

on the edge of the building just to show how cool
he was, taking his shirt and pants off first as if
there was no chill to the air. Maybe it was the smoke

held tight in his lungs, that throbbing and the way
it went shivering out through his chest and shoulders
that made him want to tear all his clothes off

and throw himself into the sun, like Icarus, exploding
over the side of the building in a wild arc of desire,
eyes fully open, chest bare and arms flung back like wings.

It must have been one of those days in March
when there are buds on the vines, a light touch
of green just outside the window—there's a breeze

and a flat wave of sun on the brick, you can see
all the different shades: red and black, the gray
and the yellow, and you want to put your skin against them,

brick as warm as an oven you'd slide loaves into
with giant paddles—a kind of wanting your whole body has:
yeast and flour, the heat and the scent, you can taste

the bread, feel the shape in your hands. But then,
being March—cold as a slap—a door opens, wind
brings water to your eyes, breath punched from your gut—

like the time I was working in the museum
with the architectural photographer. He wasn't tall,
very quiet and slender, I didn't even realize at first

I was looking at the way his trousers hung,
the way his shirt fell away from his throat and the shadow
that was left at the collarbone, right

at the base, where the soft hair was. And all of a sudden
there's this warmth going through me,
I felt my nude body on the granite slab

next to Lachaise's great bare-breasted woman,
with the wishing pond and the pennies glinting, light
sifting down through the leaves in patches—

a complete universe in every flicker—
like when there's a partial eclipse and through
each tiny pinhole in a piece of cardboard

you can see the sun, the moon and its delicious crescent
dancing in a twilight of fleeting equilibrium,
two bodies, light and dark, pressed together.

But the cold of the huge cold moon
passed over, came up to meet me,
right in the face, rude as a sidewalk—

I'm a married woman. I could taste the chill
of the granite, like the bitter aluminum you get
in your mouth when you trip, badly, or almost get smashed

by a car, fear surges up in a flood and
you gulp it back to that dark place. I've read
how in medieval times people would throw themselves

from cliffs when the light waned, how they saw the moon
cutting the sphere, the dark outline moving slowly over gold
and there was nothing left for them, no illusion

of life anymore—consumed with yearning
they felt the last long kiss of sun on their skin
as they raised their arms and they fell.

Girl in a One-Room Apartment

Because, when her boyfriend slams his fist
through the wall, the arm of the turntable

lifts, starts at the beginning again, the girl
moves one inch closer to the bathroom,

tightens her grip on the front of her robe.
Because she sees the small bathroom window,

open, night with no moon, she centers herself
between the bed and the end table,

smacks the lamp to the floor.
She hears a bulb's hollow pop.

Because his clothes, bags, and bottles
are strewn about like an animal's guts,

and he's stumbling in the dark,
she leaps, strong now, over the couch.

Because the inside of the bathroom door
is cool on her cheek, the lock

slides home loud as a .45,
the shot blown, blank.

West Chelsea

I am going to leave the city tonight,
the handball courts and the Gemini Diner,
I am going to forget about east 33rd street,
the penthouse, the Rawhide, the banks of elevators,
I want to forget the route of the C train,
the smell of the tracks when you jump down
to cross them, I want to fall asleep
and not dream of multitudes, I want to forget
that on West Fourth and Hudson my friend
held his forehead together with his hands,
I am going to abandon my FDNY cap
on top of a hydrant in alphabet city,
my Lucite stilettos on a shrine in the Bronx,
I want nothing but horizontal lines
so I don't have to get on my knees in the intersection,
I am going to pick up my body and move it
to a town where the streets are perfectly logical,
I am going to drive east on the LIE
until the only rumble is in the pit of my stomach,
I am going to shred all my take-out menus,
I am going to eat dinner at six o'clock,
I am going to be a loser and love it—
get in my car and drive east to the ocean,
until I can't stand the silence
and have to come home.

Confirmation

It is the tall transvestite in thigh-high stockings
crossing Ninth Avenue against traffic

who will save me. Celestial beehive,
a piety of pearls, white patent clutch,

the way she tugs at the hem of her skirt.
I revel in the wrist of her fine left hand—

royal, precise as a paisley headscarf
and twelve-button cardigan. Yes: there's Mary-rage

in the off-duty taxicabs, but God bless
the satin of born-again swagger,

tight little girdle of Harlequin romance
beating its way over broken asphalt,

her Chinese-red, set aglow with votives—
nary a single look over her shoulder.

Shells

"Grandmother's Toenails," the shells we found
on Hay Beach, were pale orange—thin and ridged.
But these were painted excruciating red.

In the trauma unit I held my friend's coat and handbag
while she caressed her mother's left big toe—
the rest of her body covered by a huge bag
with air pumped in to keep her warm.
Her head was swollen, bloodied at the back
where the contusion was—her neck braced,
arms tucked in for warmth. Yet there they were:
ten perfect toes. The red so red it was almost blue.

As we stood around the elevated bed,
and my friend bent the knuckle with her thumb
so carefully, the toe the center of our living universe,
we remembered what the police had said
when they gave us her possessions—the single
pearl earring, seventy-one cents from her purse,
and the little potted plant she clutched as she fell
down the stairs of the needlepoint shop and her head
hit the wall and her skull filled with blood—

we remembered they said she hadn't cried out.
And the blood was the color of fingernail polish
and the polish was the color of the small tight buds
and the buds were the size of her pedicured toenails,
and I heard my friend saying over and over:
Mamma, I'm here, I'm here now.
Eventually there was nothing we could do.
Eventually the toenails, her hardy chrysanthemums,
were the only thing left of her armor,
like shells flung aside by small invertebrates
returning to the sea in their vulnerable form—
small, soft creatures. And then
the ridges begin and the opalescent shine.

The Spool

Pantsuits, dirndl skirts, rompers, evening gowns—
she's at it again, up at night at the dining room table
with the sewing machine, tiny light blazing,
the straight pins a spray of metal in her teeth.
The whole house is still, only the snip of her shears,
the machine whining. I'm supposed to be in bed
yet I watch her night after night as she feeds the silk
beneath the metal foot of the ancient Singer, or spins
on its cranky axis the size-six mannequin (her perfect replica),
wheeled out of the closet, spins like an awkward dance partner
the muslin Cinderella. *If you look good you feel good—*

When I put on a new dress it always feels heady, secretive,
like night time, like the serious hush of the dark apartment,
the swish of chiffon twirling over parquet.
When I put on a new dress I am so much like her, trusting
an outfit to transform my life, to keep it buoyant
the way a gored skirt swings, or to keep me steady
with dependable gabardine, resilient twill.
Did she wear all those dresses? In her dreams,
at least, they were there at the ready—a corps of admirers
flattering her every move. *How fast can you sew?*
The insistent motor, mother's foot on the pedal—
she is basting a hem, she is tacking back facing,
she's putting some ease in the gather of a skirt.
Sewing until the spool runs out.

Doves

A battery of playful kisses: pecks
as carefree and frivolous as foreplay
grew more pointed while the female weakened—
eyes half-lidded, neck ruffled, damp—
breaths few and feeble.

Then she stepped away from the male—
looked about the narrow ledge, into new green
gingko branches, shrugged, smoothed herself
and took off—clean as she wanted to be.
Her tail: a delicate, upturned fan.

Rope

The girl's father laughs a little too hard
when I say: *She knows what's important in life*
as his daughter whips the dime store jump rope
over her head for the twelve thousandth time—
laughs as if I'm joking, when really, she has it down—
sparkly pink handles grimy with effort,
her face obscured by her hair, shins thin and bruised,
socks down at the ankles. Abandoned
by the rest of the crowd, the concrete square
an archipelago, an alignment with rigor the others
cannot fathom, she moves with fierce persistence
into afternoon, the heft of the handles, smack of the rope—
no Double Dutch, limbo, no communal game,
but this resolute definition of rhythm,
slatted bench shadows lengthening into space,
the other kids simply forgetting she's there,
her solitary corner of the playground darkening
as the dinner hour approaches, while pigeons pause
on their branches, squirrels come down the trunk and stop,
with rush hour beyond the fence, cars idling,
and the rope's metronome, forgotten as breath,
weaving all the disparate energies of girl—
elation, fury, eagerness, song—
into one singular strand.

2

Last Call

On the stoop steps: jolts of hormonal energy
refuse the clock on the windowsill—3:49—
and the sheer number makes it impossible to distinguish
siren, bully, ass-kisser, clown,
the one who shouts how in third grade he weighed 83 pounds—
third fucking grade I'm telling you man—
and the YO YO YO of some female in the higher extremities—

There is nothing like a porch light or a car to upset them,
someone yells *Shut Up*, there's a glass bottle—POP—
and a boy's voice goes deeper: What You Want, BITCH?
Believe it: Third. Fucking. Grade.

You want to throw a shoe but hesitate.
Sudden, romantic nostalgia: the lack of regard!
Unfettered, gyrating, yet to be chastened—
when the cops come it's you they're moving down the street,
industrious tongue, jeans straining the crotch,
vagrant, sequined, ravished, robbed.

Big Yard

Antennas, office skyline, razor wire
coiled on a slant all around the top
of the roof wall, a mile to the pavement.
Some kids call it recess. We called it Big Yard.
Something, we imagined, like back yards—
all that open air.

Once, when Valerie Butoni had me flush on the wall—
raze of raw concrete on the back of my arms,
sirens, jackhammers, garbage trucks on Lexington—
in that moment I was memorizing soot:
square black flakes like fat urban butterflies—

and pigeons: greasy, with their emerald necks, those pigeon-
blood eyes, feet like scored wire. How could one kid
own the bench, the swings, the water fountain,
the breath in my lungs?
                    In the grip of power
you might as well, if she told you to,
hurl yourself down.

Chicken

was crucial to the Scarsdale Diet—and despite Miss Trevor,
staunch vegetarian, appalled—I sucked down whole birds.
Intricate ribs, dense gray thighbones, the way
dark tendons fell away—who cares if the diet was useless?
I was fourteen, I'd just lost my innocence.
Giddy from grease, protein and hormones,
the heat of the city playground in August
and the thrill of Miss Trevor's frank disdain,

I was tossing gristle on a pile, licking my fingertips,
nothing but chicken and boys to devour:
Robert and Frankie, Skip and McVey—
seeing the world through a haze of roast meat—
all those boys, all that warm flesh, sinew and fat,
juice on my lips, those piles of shiny bones.

Adonis Garage (1978)

Drag empresses in the powder room raged.
2 A.M.: more liner, laméd lips. Thursdays

only divas, bucks, and boys in shorts got in:
scant army surplus, fur, a satin

labyrinth of lambs and lechers wound
through halls that stank of cum, the neon moon came down

and sweat, confetti, frills, and poppers fueled
the mirrored ballroom as our lewd dream unfurled.

On the balcony before the dawn horns crowed,
each glam cage spilled its gaudy, golden load

into the aisles. Oh rippling cascade—
even if we didn't win, we played.

Immortality

Who first suggested Bernie's on Sixth Avenue for nitrous oxide?
Who knew that if you jump into the tracks
there's room between the cars and the wall
if you squeeze all your breath out and mind the rats?
Who calculated the ratio, who first tested it out,
who shot the straightest? Strung up all those tiny lights
so the house looked like a brothel or an Indian restaurant?
Who suggested the party move downtown,
that we stop the elevator between floors
(the girl began to weep)? Who left me alone
with a bag and some works in a too bright bathroom,
searching for my vein?

Who pried that deadbolt open with a crowbar—
what was her name? The one who spread her jacket
like a net? Who never lied?
Who told me Ian cut his wrists in a bathroom
lit with a thousand candles, that if he hadn't done it
he probably would have killed us all instead.

A Door Opens

Saturday rainbow street fair in Chelsea,
first sign of summer, mesh shirts and royal abs,
and when I pass the Rawhide bar—bare folded muscle arms
on a bare chest, smell of vented smoke and
raw beer, a sign up for 7:30 Go-Go Men—

I think of you back then—Beach Boy Cocktail Hour—
after hours in the new gay Mecca, seventies rampage—
twirling newfound disco delirium, mirrored balls,
sweat, poppers, leather G-string—explosions
of chest, mouth, anonymous cock—I think of you,

Navy virgin until twenty-five, your brief
naïve marriage in a chantilly punchbowl, then unbound
from wife and child, Baptist choir halitosis,
two-bedroom dinner party silver patterns
and the sanctity of white buttered broccoli—

Emancipation! A floor-through walk-up and
long tan limbs nightly, orchids by the bucketful,
House Beautiful Plexiglas chrome double-suede.
And where was I while you danced in red sequins
until morning? Cutting the knotted, bloody cord:

you at Anvil, me in the East Village, anonymous
stall fucks, gold glory riot of thrust and blow, fishnet
confetti, busboys and bus station spring chicken,
mink handcuffs, shower of semen.
All this was before the new cancer,

before Paul's shriveled limbs and pharmaceuticals,
before the New Mexico carrot juice enema shrine,
before Michele curled sick in the shadow
of an East Side light bulb broom closet,
Jimmy surrounded by calla lilies.

Who marks the pale forehead with ash? Velvet ropes
released as the censer sways. Reprieved,
consoling the death of others, you're out of it all,
still beautiful survivor—no lesions, no slat-counting ribs,
Long Island two-car suburban sagging poolside.

And me? Your daughter by appointment only?
Your distant relation, your biggest fan?
I'm safely through college and AA church basements.
My children swipe your reading glasses,
make jokes about your bald spot.

Yet it comes back in summer—
flash of bare-chested thump,
the occasional breath of holy sweat
triple-X. A pierced nipple, a door opens.
Oh miraculous dark room beyond.

Meat District

Against the loading dock and open trucks, the boy
steps from the curb, a girl. More slender, though,
with a higher ass. All of seventeen, he bends
into the window of a Town Car, leather trench,
black fishnets, pumps. He doesn't take the ride.
He puts his fingers to his lips then draws them smooth
along the windshield, winking as it speeds away.

Reflections in Porcelain

This was my gig: white lace apron,
cut-out bra and crop. I crouched above him
every Thursday in the marble bathroom,
pissed on his bare chest and let him lick me dry.
He wasn't the first to love the thought
of the redness of a bottom, mark of a heel.

So when my ex dropped three tabs of sunshine
and decided I'd screwed his best friend,
I thought I knew what to expect. Hadn't
the drag queen across the street, pistol-whipped,
sat silent on her folded raincoat? *There is nothing*
anyone can do she said, and the bistro patrons
hailed their cabs and stepped around her.

And when he held me dangling over West End,
window wide onto the avenue, I know the woman
outside the building with her collar open, back to God,
heard me get it as I prayed for one less smack against the sill.

While Watching the Star-Spangled Banner

I might have rolled toward the edge of the futon, I might
have let my leg or my arm fall to the floor, watching
him walk, naked, to the telephone and back.
She, on the other side, near the wall, was pale, nodding
in and out, scratching her white thighs.

A tiny, cheap apartment: wall-to-wall junk. Odd woman out
in our ménage, I dreamed —when I could be that focused—
that she would find another gig, lose her house keys, lose
her way home in the scrawl of night. I wanted to be the only one
on the bed. She looked so tired, her small body swollen, she
hit up against me and sighed with a delicious fury at the end
of her long breath as if she'd frankly given up and died—
and of all the freaky, wacked-out things, the night I left,
she did.

Surrender

Once, early Sunday morning, bounding from bar to bar,
I saw, on a wire-mesh trash can, on top of a cascade
of coffee cups, strip club flyers, flayed umbrellas,
resting in a tinfoil rosette, an uneaten bagel:
perfect, pale, abandoned.
Looking left then right, like a fugitive,
I took the bread in my hand, soft and pristine, stuffed it
in my coat pocket, kept on walking down First Avenue.
Now I could ask the man on the flattened box
to move over, I could slide down slick as a wet leaf,
no more thresholds, grow my toenails, mutter into my chest,
the city was mine. As if I'd cut the last tether—
I was free to scratch my crotch, be unkempt
in plain view, glory in the rat's nest,
all doorways open, all vestibules—
every last paradise open to me.

Fierce-Throated Beauty

He had a gap between his front teeth wide enough
to slide a quarter through. I could imagine him
producing the coin from behind his ear
like some sideshow magician then pressing it out
through his teeth with his tongue. Funny thing was,

if you saw him on the street he would duck—
pretend to be scanning a movie marquee, perusing
the specials on a Chinese menu. But get him going
and he'd sputter in excitement, lean so close
you could see yourself in his baldness, and if you told him

you were down that day he would take out a pad
from his left vest pocket and write a few lines—
Blake, Cavafy, Milton, Pessoa—he'd scrawl them out
and dispense the page like a doctor's prescription, folding
the paper as he slid it across the table as if poetry

could blind you. He had a guardian angel
who sat on his refrigerator and screamed at him in Yiddish.
She kept him safe, he said, from fried food and Republicans,
from small dogs and middle-aged vegetarian women.
Once he led a conga line of perfect strangers around a park

on Bleecker Street singing Whitman: "To a Locomotive in Winter."
An arthritic park attendant had this look on his face—
as he swung around at the end of the line I thought he might die
from joy. One small girl running in circles like a shitzu pup,
squealing "fierce-throated beauty!"—her nanny glanced at the sky

in trepidation. It was the day of the Gay Pride Parade:
singing nuns led the Leather Lesbians down Christopher.
That night we stood on a fire escape,
some open mike reading where the Mateus was free.
He barely came up to my shoulder, and yet

from the height of my stilettos I swore he was the champion
of my nineteen years—drunk, misunderstood as I was
by the whole living world. And in truth,
he was my angel that summer: early eighties,
the year of the green fur coat and asymmetrical hair.

On the fire escape he helped me off with my shoes
and from what I remember, back on with my dignity—
down the crowded stairwell to the avenue. He let me
finish my soggy paean, never once making a play
for his Freshman Comp teacher's aid—this sorry girl

with neon mascara and a dog-eared *Duino Elegies*.
If a gun's on the wall it'll go off by the last act
he said, quoting Chekhov. His father had died with his head
in his own piss and he said this thinking it would save me.
Thing is you can barely hear a .45 on a summer night

in the Village. He didn't say a word about my "condition,"
just found me a cab. It was raining. And of course the gun
did go off—several years and many drunk cab rides later.
Not the genteel tap-tap of room service—a gunshot
blasts the door from its hinges, wood cracks and splinters,

it hurls us from our beds to the cold
motel floor, loss written in red, floor to ceiling,
across the bathroom wall and nothing is left
but the stink of spent powder, black shards of glass,
a kind of fury even angels can't walk through.

The Amusement Park

Every night I dreamed of The Cyclone.
Siren blues, reds of surrender.
Up from the subway, cotton candy
sea-light spun around me
until I was sticky, captured like a fly.

The woman with the spangled torso whispered;
snakes oozed like butter through a sieve.
I followed the maudlin impresario
whose monkey wore an Austrian monocle
and baited the diamondback boys on the boardwalk.

A man barked; I stepped up to the line.
Entering through a wide-open mouth
past wicked incisors, infants impaled,
I too swallowed the flaming daggers,
was submerged in oil, felt nails on my tongue.

Every night I dreamed of The Cyclone
and here I was, the bloodshot eye of it:
flung against a red vinyl seat
with a force that married chrome and wind,
leaving my small change behind.

2D12365690

Sirens on Eighth Avenue—a fire, an explosion, what did it matter?
—in those days, in the room so small I could barely turn,
I would light the oven and sit on a footstool
in front of the open door, red coil like neon under the racks.

I stared at it for hours—a fireplace, as in big-family houses—
into the mouth of that contentment, the room so cold
my head would drop toward the dusty heat, my shirt pulled down
over my rosy knees, until I fell asleep on the footstool

and when I turned from the stove I felt the bald chill,
when I walked by the liquor store I got a pang of remorse,
when I passed the deli's steamy windows, no denying
my scorched forelock, my branded forehead:
General Electric, Louisville, KY., 2D12365690.

Hep C

On West 24th I uncovered my anger.
Raw brick and batten, three flights up
with a great view of nowhere, it was there
I pulled my hard little chair to the wall,
went unshowered for weeks, shrank from all mirrors,
where I spit on the floor, learned to love a straight razor,
me with my sleeve rolled up past my elbow,
my peppermints and my parochial skirt,
my fingerless gloves and my dented spoon.

This was years before my liver renounced me—
solid, shapeless slug
that sucked everything up like a sex-starved chaperone,
bloodbuddy with everyone in our nasty little neighborhood,
my royal big sister, ponderous watchdog—
enraged at having had to live my life.

Positive

1. READING THE RESULTS

I don't move,
but the inside corner
of my right eye turns glassy,
then shatters,

hands focus more sharply.

I don't move,
but the pigeon shudders
on the sill.

The door opens to a maze
of wallpaper, family photos—
their bliss-frieze burns
the last unaffected corner of my sight,
like molten Karo.

My husband's mouth collapses,
and the air about his shoulders
has crystallized.
We don't say a word,
all the noise is around us,
the letter, half-folded, on the desk,
an albatross, a dove.

2. POSITIVE

Because in those days there were no words
for such things I took handfuls of vitamins and slept
with a trumpet flower under my pillow, I ate
at the Kiev on Second Avenue at four every morning:
enormous boiled potato pierogis shivering in pools
of butter, little sides of sautéed onions, paper cups of pure
sour cream, Dr. Brown's Cel-Ray, no ice, as chaser,

but now when the call comes I'm sitting in the kitchen
with two plastic funnels over my breasts and the pump
on the counter with its hydraulic suck and the cast iron
sputtering of eggs, the kids already bickering at table,
milk flowing into baby bottles, even now the word
heroin makes me feel the lovely way
a body can go slack from inside out.

3. A SINGLE DROP

I'd never paid much mind
to my implements, but now
I paint "Fire Engine Red"

on the handle of my razor, a single drop
on my nail clippers, one long
stroke on my lethal toothbrush

to cordon off my blood,
I tend and sop each splash or seep,
soiled band-aids, love-smeared sheets—

every bleeding gum, torn hangnail,
paper cut, scrape, gully of cracked lip
another hazard, each

infectious throb now
forever watched as I patrol
my body's raging arroyo

in the family bathroom,
to keep my children
safe from me.

4. PAPER GOWNS

X-rays, lab coat, and me wearing
those delicate petals (gaping,
cold through the sleeves).
He asks me to extend my palms:
the motion is of pushing away.
Breathe with your mouth, he says, soft
tup, tup, tup, along my spine,
as if checking a cantaloupe.

There is a piece of gum
beneath the windowsill,
green imprint of a thumb.
We're talking percentages, genotypes,
we're talking bundled pharmaceuticals.
Studies, it seems, are inconclusive.

I try to look at the big picture:
a talc-free rubber glove at the edge of the trash,
neither in, nor out. On the insurance card,
raised numbers, black ink worn away.
There's a girl on the street with her head back,
the strap of her dress falling carelessly.

3

A Fairy Tale

Come in my boy.
He lays down his wares
as I light the oven, heat
fills the room.

So easy: the full set
unrolls in its red cloth, softly,
no clinking, like a royal carpet,
a felt bed of jewels.

Had I thought about cleavers,
kitchen shears, boning knives
before this nineteen-year-old
rang my bell? He starts

by cutting a penny in streamers.
Then he lays down
a length of rope, has me
slice it in two with one stroke.

So easy. Next,
shoe leather, no match for us:
dark brown strips
tenderloin on my kitchen table.

Note the blend of carbon and stainless steel.
I lean back, flick my thumb on the edge:
prick, prick, prick.
My stove is as big as a man.

Oh wily birds, my allies,
eaters of breadcrumbs,
you take poor Gretel, thin
as she is, up the marzipan stairs.

I'll take the galley set
and bonus shears, each handle
with its three perfect rivets,
my smile like the glint on a long blade.

In the Window of the DV8 Store Near My House

From the display of cock rings, neoprene gloves,
spiked collars, whips, and latex nurse's uniforms,
what mesmerizes my three-year-old
is the black rubber mask with tiny eye slits and a pig's snout.
I tell her grownups play games sometimes too.

She is standing in her stroller by now, her face and fingers
smearing the glass as we watch businessmen
move from case to case, uneasy with this child
who stares and waves through the pane,
through the legs of a pig man.
She is watching them. They watch me.
I am watching them watch her watch me
watch them and the pig watches us all
from the white behind his eye slits.

How do I tell her that sometimes you love
and hate at once? That there will be
serious games of hide and seek, you'll want
the bad guy to tie you to a stake, and also want
the prince to burst in and save you—

the policeman from the neighborhood
coming up now to stand beside the two of us,
gun bulging, smiles—a welter of good and bad
like a slap on a bare behind—something stronger
than love, stronger than punishment—always
there, inside me: pig snout with a ring of gold.

The Object

1.

Watered-down green, like an aftershock
of emerald, the object cast in a perfect arc
from the shoulder of the highway

with the force of the heaving but also easy
as the air that held it, a singular thing—thrown
by its thin neck, not a bird, not a bat, but a bottle,

like a Molotov cocktail, only this, being empty,
container of pure intent, was beautiful, light
through the long fluted torso, the delicate waist.

As if glad to be free of its launchers—
the half-hidden band of boys at the roadside—
it sailed in lazy cartwheels, one revolution

leading the next, thoughtful, elegant as a wheel,
the thick round base propelling it forward, hitting
its peak above the center lane and then starting down,

almost reluctantly. And the whole day slowed:
trees by the highway, their bare arms waving foolishly,
the self-important cars, fine dilations of glass.

2.

When the bottle struck
the broad curve of the windshield,
point of impact spiraling outward in a web of cracks,
the whole window clouded, glass
drifting a fine mist down—
dashboard, steering wheel, stick shift
glinting like a sunlit lake.

3.

The fine lacework canopy of shattered glass
suspended above—slightly bowed, shivering—

we waited for the heavy sheet to fall,
and whatever we had been fighting about while we drove

hung there too as we pulled off
and sat on the edge of the highway, the other cars

hissing, traveling faster than we thought possible.
I picked a tiny splinter from the collar of my coat.

A small bird—a house sparrow—landed on a branch,
the radio all of a sudden very loud.

Rust

Listen to that pleading: high, incessant—
someone's bad brakes plying Eighth Avenue's whole
unholy length. When he coughs,

rooms away, I know the ratio:
wet to dry. Nicotine lung-shudder.
It passes and there is merely street again.

The first night he slept apart from me
I counted seven coughs, two curses,
thirteen throat-clearings.

The first night he slept apart from me
I still slept nude. There is a door
and beyond that door a perfect

little garden. Hinges
underused until
they've rusted shut.

Anniversary

As though a rose should shut, and be a bud again.—*John Keats*

1. SPONTANEOUS COMBUSTION

It all comes around to the yearning:
even the mortars and small artillery,
even the silence. Something small
in the place below the sternum
is ravenous, always, would even feed upon itself.

The couple in the corner booth at Blimpie's
ignore their coffee. He is smoking.
She is leaning toward him, bare knees, bright lips,
smoothing the petal of her damp handkerchief.

Like the first boy, how he looked at me.
Even as I pretended to be sleeping, even as I felt avenues
being torn apart and repaired in the night
with sirens flashing red and yellow.

There are times when the gulf between the mind and the body
is so vast—my bright red lipstick is nothing but a ruse,
a way to keep the vinyl banquette from bursting into flames—

2. IN PRAISE OF THE REAGAN ERA

If we could go backward—
start with our darkness: two bodies in bed,
two separate galaxies, cold and unknown.

If we could go from bed to table—
plates still warm—an evening unbroken,
tears safe in their ducts, all venom swallowed,

work our way through the toast flying
into your hand and you placing it back,
precisely, on the plate.

Back through decades, to the initial lapse,
head turned away, through the glance at the floor
back to the little love song we used to sing

gathering in the back of my throat,
to a door flung open—fields of new grass—
where I'd walk out with my future behind me.

3. ALTIPLANO

She never looked at the map,
he never said where they were going.
Instead, one silent meal after the other:
piles of hard blue potatoes, freeze-dried
on the altiplano, salty coffee.
The locals ate sheep's heads,
plucking out the eyes with great relish.

Eat something, for God's sake,
you look like a starved dog.
Don't touch me.
I feel like I'm going to die here.

Then nothing.
Then nothing.

The road went higher until the vegetation stopped.
In La Paz he bought a dried llama fetus,
reputed to bring good luck, and brought it home
in a newspaper. She placed it over their front door.
And all the bugs in its tight, collapsed chest
started their warm journey outward.

4. ARCHITECTURE

Whoever put that enormous asterisk of duct tape over the window
may not have seen the layers of blue adhesive refracting
and plunging into its own fierce geometry
like a galaxy burst into being,
a wild combination of need and material,
energy and architecture.
One heavy wind, you know it's going to slip,
one screen door slam—

It's like when he came home and said he lost his job—
all those sharp little edges protruding
but the tape doing its best to hold things together,
sticky strips a kind of spit and glue—

Little pockets of air, little pockets of glass,
like those dark internal organs that hold and hold and hold
until they don't.
The biggest shard is hanging there, a guillotine.
On the other side of the glass is just more air, patient
and sinister, bringing the pane down in tiny increments—

5. THE SEED

They've begun to merge, those lakeside summers,
softening, every year, like graceful umlauts
over *u* or *i:* all rain or too much sun or
when the kids hijacked the sprinkler. Now
their boundaries ooze, berries into jam,
sweet and viscous as one season
leaves off slowly (robins, dew, wet sand)
where the next begins. But that single summer
stays taut and whole, firmly lodged
in a recess behind the mind, some hole
where grief catches, out of reach:
a blackberry seed, ground down between the teeth.

6. ISLANDS

Bruised purple leaves, soil made from blossom,
the strange yellow mushrooms that appear
overnight—it's as if she were standing on the edge
of a thought that would draw all the strands into one.

And he, after preparing the kindling, a perfect tower
over leaves and scrap paper—triage, consolidation—
goes through a door in the privet hedge,
and the light shifts.

There is nothing behind her eyes anymore.
No room, no sunlight, no green grass.
It's like the runoff from the road, each storm
the silt comes further underneath the door.

Back now at his task: the present, the garden, the fire
where he places the grill and the fish, gills falling open,
the mouths, the articulate jaws set, as if sewn.

The bruise will go from black to blue to yellow.

7. BEYOND AESTHETICS (SCHUNNEMUNK FORK)

Enormous planes of steel, four of them,
cut into the small hill: one every hundred yards or so.
So simple as we approach from the sunny side,
morning east, metal flat and uninflected, simple
as razor blades in the grass. At first we aren't sure
what to make of them—is this really it?
Form imposed upon nature so smoothly?
It is only as we move along in our steady, silent,
little green tourist tram that we see the way the sun
hits the side of the steel and leaves a knife shadow
on the ground on the other side. We pass
in our methodical way, we see beyond the weathering steel,
it's the shadow that makes the sculpture.

8. ANNIVERSARY

Solitude in a headlock: cumulative rash
beneath a wedding ring: gravity: crease-riven forehead:
weight of a sleeping body on a mattress:
practice smile: practice laugh: newspaper on the floor:
door slam: Chinese containers: grease-spattered bills:
teakettle scream: keys flung at a wall:
hammer and nail: nail disappearing:

remember, in the Chinese restaurant,
the honeyed walnuts and perfect bowl of rice?
How the steam from a cup framed your face?
Remember the longest day—our summer like a bride,
barefoot on the verge of a forest?

9. SARDINES

She dreamed of separating his head from his body.

But in the moment she always grew distracted or optimistic,
the F train would pass in front of their apartment
and sardines would cry out from their tins,
rattling the cabinets with such ferocity
she could do nothing but grasp the sorry
edge of the mattress and pray for a natural disaster.
There was Drano bubbling in the sink,
a kid upstairs with a Bongo Board.
No one should get decapitated in Brooklyn
without an anthem, and all the bards were busy,
serenading newborns or beautiful women.
Some hairspray is Ultra-Maximum-Hold,
you can practically shellac your life to the wall.

10. DIVORCE

Once the word has been flung out, it lives
on its own, on the table—like a birth, like a door
burst open—its V a wedge, hammered
into wood, the final consonant hissing, sibilant.

So when he asks how am I feeling—when he asks
what news do I bring to that table
where we sit, staring at a clotted salt shaker,
a plate of fried eggs and a dead geranium,

after having a night to test my tongue on the word,
I say *oh fine*—
all the while holding that *O* in my mouth
like a cool pearl, and that *I*
growing, lengthening—

11. HIS COLLARBONE

Certain as a constellation,
a promontory, an invitation.

There was no hope for me,
standing at a window in a bathrobe:

it would always sing, like a tuning fork,
it would try to break free, to reinforce its nobility,
it would strain against weather and against the flesh of women,
it would shift in relation to the other bones, swell and shrink,
like a candle in a dark hall it would taunt me
with its elegance,
it would tear through the paper surrounding it,
it would set the paper on fire—
burning in the night, in the middle
of the week: it would ignite the dishtowel
and the shower curtain,
it would incite the ficus to flame.

Or is it a flame, a beacon—
the boat my utterly sexual body,
his collarbone a light above the dark water?

12. WINTER

On the mantlepiece—how many little objects there are,
end to end: the rusted horseshoe from Colombia,
wooden triptych from Spain,
tiny vial of holy water from the River Jordan,
the snapshot of you on the Hudson with the towers
still intact, candlesticks that used to be part
of other pairs—the press of things
on this narrow ledge—a small gold Buddha
pushed behind a pinwheel made of Popsicle sticks,
postcard of the cat "Born Blind,"
the Greenwich Village Little League trophy,
each vying for its place in the landscape of our attention,
things pushed to the back now coming forward—

I start with a wedding gift, the stuffed Atlantic seagull.
That head, so long and narrow, peering
over its shoulder like a cornered thing.
I ease the bird down to the salt-white curb.

The Plant

In the water-ringed, chipped clay pot by the window:
the aloe-vera plant I've raised for decades,
a gift from my husband, who gave it to me wrapped
in a wad of wet paper towel, young and green, brilliant
green, a mere sprig, spotted white like a fawn
and oozing clear and slightly sticky from its cut end,
little spines belying its soft, exposed middle,
young, but slightly arrogant, the way the young are.
And although I doubted a tree would develop,
I stuck a stick in the soil, twined up her length,
gave her a pot of her own, some space by the radiator,
Miracle Gro and two cups of water,
until the white spine tips, like little candles,
little flames, began to glow on all sides—
I believed she was thriving.

Now the whole plant has keeled over.
I tried restaking, spraying, tamping down the soil
only nothing works, the plant's gone limp—
Oh my lively little lettuce,
green is the green defeat of boiled spinach,
I lift you up with a single finger—
how many others are like you, failing to put down roots
or with roots so elaborately twisted
in their tiny plastic pots they strangle themselves?

Was I mistaken, or had you lifted your arms in
optimism? What has become of you,
my sapling, my live wire, lithe wire,
stump of a spawn of a redwood that nestled in my soul,
soul of a redwood that furrowed in my soil?

Appetite

The merest suggestion of mouth
and I was ravenous—I filled the house
with chocolate, chestnuts, strudel,
blood sausage; I bathed in butter.

A glimpse of tongue and I was undone,
simply a hint of heavy cream
and the wax came off in a greasy slab,
there were no cauldrons large enough.

I imagined his body drawn in sections,
flank, ribs, and tenderloin, I rubbed
the blade to sparks, my stove walls
sweated, windows dripping.

Afterwards the house was a shell.
My tongue: scorched white.
I had to staple my stomach
down to the size of a lichee nut.

Thimbleful of broth, thimbleful
of gruel, the merest suggestion
floods my mouth with memory
so rich I practically drown.

Although We Are Legally Separated My Husband Pulls Me into the Bathroom and Kisses Me

No excuse—none exists. Leftward tilt
of head, long look held one beat more—
a door left open "by mistake." Strong or
weak, we know each other's ream of guilt.
Pressed against the cabinet he built
when I was pregnant, we frantically explore
again, the volt that runs, a twisted cord,
between us. Who was it left, who really jilted
whom? The body leaves a dearth of clues,
a wealth of want; the crooked mirror's clouded
with our breath, our need, our sorrow. I lose
the lover of my grown-up life, and now he
burns—a phantom limb, a fevered ruse
that makes me hurt, then makes me (hurting) doubt it.

In the Course of Unwinding

In the slow unraveling of a marriage
one can feel the draft at odd moments,
like the shirt too short when you bend over,
the way it rides up, exposing that whole warm
private terrain at the small of the back.
(When did this shirt get too small anyway?).
There are snags, places where the fabric pulls
and catches, the comfortable folds and pleats
worn thin give way and you're standing there
with your skin in the raw breeze—

There are moments when the static snaps,
little lights going off, synapses firing in the body's brain
creating a new lightness, limbs
with the feel of new limbs, hair standing up
on the back of the neck and even the underparts,
nipples tightening against the cold, shoulders tightening,
the body a great statue unveiled, a new bronze figure
leaning into the elements, awaiting its patina,
its patience, its birdshit, its snow.

But the unwinding. It begins from the inside.
At first nothing more than a shifting, motion
deep beneath a calm and familiar surface,
like a shifting of tectonic plates,
or an uncoiling, undulating, like a tide, shifting,
and all the separate stitches, all the threads
rubbing against each other, all the ribs
and the purls and the seams, the dropped sleeves
and the damp mohair and the scratchy wool easing,
the yarn unraveling and the spool in the center
twirling on its axis like a shy ballerina—

I remember how it felt to stand naked on the rock
with water in front of me, pounding water,
bruises on my body and no one there to see them,
and the freedom of the first foot lowered
toward the cold spring, mist hitting rock
and the diffusion like a cloud, a rainbow, a veil,
I remember the sight of my body in the forest,
how it didn't resemble any of its surroundings,
only glowed, stronger than I'd thought possible,
how it felt to stand ready on the rock,
how deep the water looked, the dark green and gray
and how I'd have to throw myself in all at once,
into the shock of engulfing, the tides,
the pull beneath the rocks,
the cold and the moss and the stones and the smaller stones,
and the little slither of fish against my skin—

In the unraveling, the slow dissolution, I remember
how it felt to stand on that rock, my body frail, white, cold,
the weariness of the journey, the many levels of water,
the firm foundation of the rocks, loving that foundation,
my clothing on the damp moss in a pile, gray, smelling rank,
smelling of the journey, the sorry, sweaty little pile,
and the ferns and the moss and the music of the water,
the movement over the stones, under the stones,
around in the glasslike eddies, the glasslike
skin of the water, the rippling charge of it—
there was no one around, there was me and the water,
my body would meet that water above and below the water,
and I knew the way it would taste on my skin.

The Forest at the Edge of the World

Today I left groceries by the playground on Hudson
and tried to haul, up toward my block,
a cross section of a maple grown too large,
chainsawed into manhole covers. Alphonso,
Super for All Buildings east of the projects,
stopped sweeping. He leaned his bald broom
against the stoop, nudged the wood with his toe.
"Nothing to do but roll it," he said, hands
deep in his pockets. I nodded,
barely believing my luck in the midst of asphalt,
transistor radios, and the wet smell of dogs
as he squatted eye level with the log, heaved it
against his shoulder like a man who bears
a handmade cross for miles on his penitent back.
I saw a kind of glory in his eyes, he understood
the heft of the trunk, nicks in the damp bark.
I stood on the side and righted the thing
and together we rolled this boulder of tree
past the Indian deli, the Russian shoe repair,
the Caribbean bakery. "You can smell the forest,"
he said, as we reached my stoop, wood
in the crook of his neck, sawdust and humus and sweat.
And we hoisted the thing, one step at a time, stopping
only to breathe the scent of sap and after a good half hour
it was filling the whole of my apartment—
the shade, the damp smell, that enormous presence—
light brown rings so perfect my whole life
fell right down inside them, concentric circles,
tree within tree, the single slab a world within itself—
suddenly it was thirty-five years ago:
I stood on the edge of a forest, someplace upstate,
and looked up into the branches of my first
true and majestic tree, in the first real forest—trees
instead of buildings. Oh the breadth of those limbs—
after the taut geometry of elevator, fire escape, lobby,

to see through branches to the sun—I believed
the world was mine, there was sap in my veins,
the tree was limitless, the scent of the tree,
the bark and the branch and the six-year-old sightline,
which goes on to the edge of the known world.

In the Prairie Schooner Book Prize in Poetry series

Cortney Davis, *Leopold's Manueuvers*
Rynn Williams, *Adonis Garage*